Gerry the Pig

Peter Gargiulo

PAGE PUBLISHING
Conneaut Lake, PA

First originally published by Page Publishing 2024

ISBN 979-8-89157-232-4 (pbk)
ISBN 979-8-89157-234-8 (digital)

Printed in the United States of America

This book is dedicated to the memory of Gerry's dear friend, Pigcasso.

Gerry would also like to dedicate this book to all the piggy sanctuaries throughout the world, like Ross Mill Farm in Jamison, Pennsylvania, that help his piggy friends live happy lives.

He would especially like to thank Brian R. Hackett, New Jersey animal rights advocate and leader. His vision and encouragement helped to make this book possible.

Hi, everyone. My name is Gerry the Pig, and I live in New Jersey with my papa and mama. They are my human parents, and I love them very much. I am a potbelly mini pig, and I was born in September 2015. Some people think that a "mini pig" or a "teacup pig" stays small. But you know what, we don't! *Oink!* We can weigh between 150 and 200 pounds. I'm about 150 pounds. I guess I can be considered mini because my piggy friends that live on farms are close to about nine hundred pounds! Those are big oinkers! Did you know that we are as smart as a four-year-old little boy or girl? Sometimes I play tricks on my papa and mama just like a little kid. When I was much smaller, I would open up the cabinet below the sink and go in and hide on my parents. They would look for me all over the house. I'd hear them calling, "Gerry, oh, Gerry, where are you?" I would laugh, but then when they would hear me grunting, they would open up the cabinet, and I would run out. *Oink!* They found me! *Oink!*

When I was a small baby piglet, my papa and I would play, and I would run around the house, then I would get tired and lay down next to my papa; and sometimes I would even sleep on top of him. Us pigs like to sleep and cuddle next to other piggies, so I guess I consider my papa to be another piggy. *Oink!* He always tells me that he is my pig papa because, even though I am a big boy now, I still sometimes sleep and cuddle next to him. I really like to snuggle under blankets. This is one of my favorite blankets that I like to sleep with. It's so warm and comfy.

Do you have a favorite blanket?

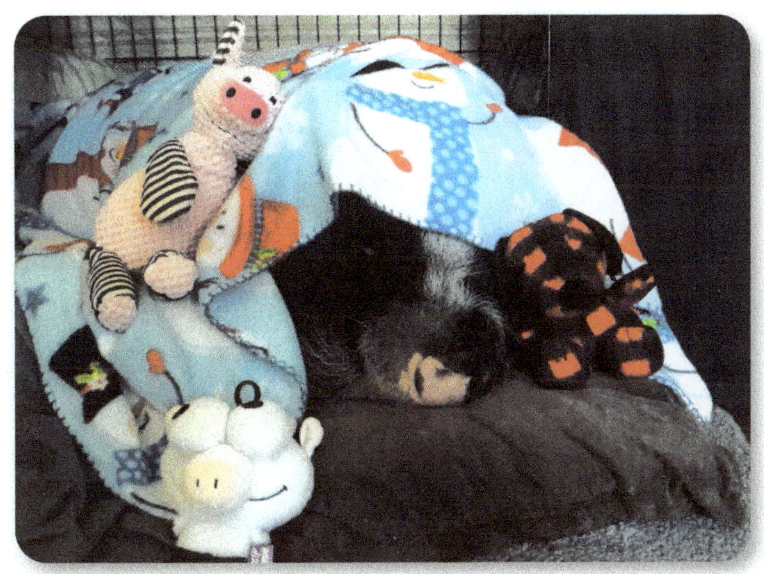

Oh! Just in case you are wondering how I am able to write this book for you using my hooves, I actually taught myself how to do it. It took a while, but I did it, and now you are reading what I typed. If you believe that you can do something, like I did, always know that if you keep trying and never give up, you will do it. *Oink!*

I live in a very nice house, and I have a yard to play in, and I have a lot of furry and feathered friends in the backyard. I have squirrel friends. I have groundhog friends. I have blue jay friends. I have grackle friends, and I have robin and cardinal friends. I love all my friends, but I think my favorite friends are the squirrels because when they eat peanuts, they always leave little pieces behind that I just happen to find and eat. Yay! Free peanuts!

Thank you, my little squirrel friends!

Oink! Oink! Here's a picture of me when I was about four months old. See how small I was? I was celebrating my first New Year with my new parents. It was January 2016.

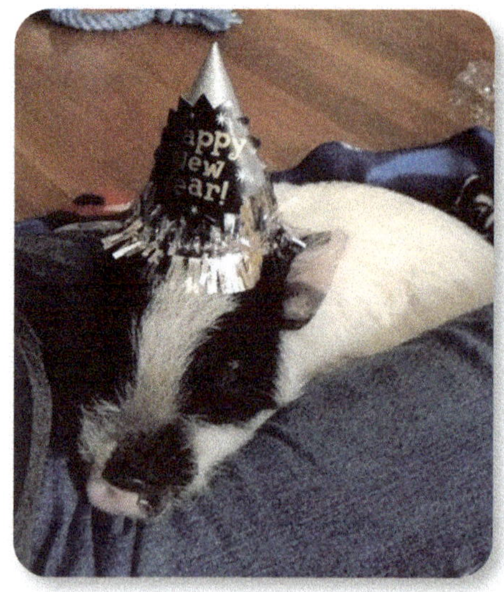

I was so tired from celebrating the night before that I slept in the next day.

When I was small, I used to run around the house like a crazy piggy. Us piggies don't have paws like my doggie friends. We have hooves, so sometimes we can slip and slide on a floor without a carpet. I remember that when I was just a little kid, I would run around the house, chasing my papa; and when I tried to stop on the wooden floor, I would go, "Wee, *oink*!" and slide across the floor. Now that I am older, and a big boy, my papa and I play in the backyard where I won't slide. We play "get the piggy." That's when he chases me around the yard, and I run really fast to get away. Then I turn around, and we play "get the papa." That's when I run back at him and chase him as fast as I can. When I catch up to him, my papa falls to his knees. I put my head under his arm, and I do a belly flop so that he can rub my belly. It's so much fun!

Oink! I love to get belly rubs.

For breakfast and dinner, I eat special mini-pig food. They look like little pellets. They are actually pretty tasty. But I'm always excited for lunch because for lunch I get a nice, big, healthy salad, with romaine lettuce, celery, zucchini, carrots, watermelon, and some olive oil. Wow! I'm getting hungry just writing about it. My papa tells people that I eat healthier than he does. When I am outside and it's lunchtime, I go to the back door and bang on it with my head, and I have a big head. That's my way of telling them "Hey, where's my lunch? I am oinken' hungry!" In the spring, summer, and fall, after I eat, I'll go back to my blanket and umbrella and lay down outside again. After I eat lunch when it is cold during the wintertime, I come back inside and snuggle under my nice warm, soft blankets.

I know...my life is so tough. *Oink!* I like when my papa lays down with me outside. He usually uses my belly as a pillow and reads his book.

When it's really hot, I like to go into my pool.

It cools me off, and the best part is that my mama puts Cheerios in the water. Once she puts the Cheerios into the water, I jump right in and eat my Cheerios that are floating in the water. I never knew Cheerios floated until I saw it with my own eyes. Actually, I would go into the pool without the Cheerios, but if I tell her that, I won't get free Cheerios to eat. *Oink!* Do you like Cheerios? They are my favorite treat!

Yes, even me, Gerry the Pig needs a "bath" sometimes. Especially after I roll around in the dirt. My parents tell me that I go from a piggy that is white with black spots to a piggy that looks grey and dirty. I used to not like taking baths, until my mama figured out a way for me to stay still while I get cleaned. She puts some peanut butter on a cutting board, and as I am being soaped up and rinsed off, I lick the peanut butter off the cutting board. Genius! Not only am I getting nice and clean so I smell nice but I am also getting free peanut butter. Now I love getting a "bath" outside. Do you like taking baths?

I have a very good piggy friend of mine that lives in South Africa. Her name is Pigcasso. She is a very famous artist that sells her paintings all over the world. I even have one of her masterpieces hanging in my living room. *Oink!*

Every once in a while, we text each other and talk about piggy things. I sometimes send her one of her favorite snacks—caramel popcorn. Yep, I even have a picture of her being fed popcorn by Joanne.

Joanne is the director of the Sanctuary, and she takes very, very good care of Pigcasso and all her animal friends at the Sanctuary. Pigcasso has cow friends, goat friends, and even other piggy friends. I like Pigcasso. I'm glad she is my friend. She lives in South Africa, so when it is summertime for me here in New Jersey, it is wintertime there; and when it is wintertime here, Pigcasso is enjoying her summer in South Africa. I hope she has a pool to have fun like I do when it gets hot in the summertime.

When it is really hot, I lie on my beach blanket in the backyard and relax after a long day of eating, sleeping, eating, and sleeping again.

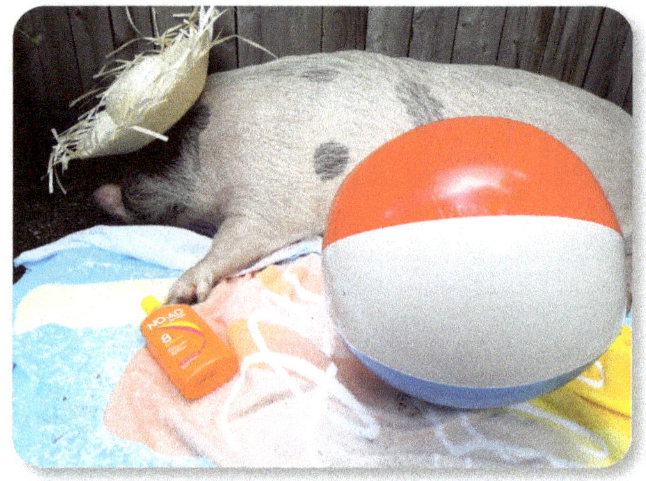

I'm just a little boy, so when it gets really sunny and hot in the summer, my papa has to put sunscreen lotion on me because I shed all my hair in the summer, and I don't want to get a sunburn.

In the wintertime, I don't go out as much because it's too cold. When it snows, I have a nice, warm jacket to wear.

I like going out into the snow. Maybe next winter when it snows a lot, I'll go out to the backyard and build a snow pig with my papa. Yay! Oink!

My papa brings sick birdies to a place called the Raptor Trust in Millington, New Jersey, where they take care of the birdies and make them better. Once they get better, they release them back into the wild so that they can live a happy birdie life. Last year, for Christmas, the Santa Piggy gave me a red-tailed hawk stuffie toy. I was so happy!

Oink!

I think once I got to see the Santa Piggy in my backyard. He was only there for a few minutes, but I was able to take a quick picture of him just before he flew away in his piggy sleigh to bring gifts to other piggies throughout the world.

Some say that Santa Pig looks like me. What do you think?

Once, a long time ago, I told my parents that when I get old enough, I wanted to move to Lancaster, Pennsylvania. I even grew a beard so that I can live on an Amish farm.

They told me that maybe someday, if I get a job and learn how to drive, I may be able to move there by myself.

I had a job this spring in a doughnut shop. But it didn't last long.

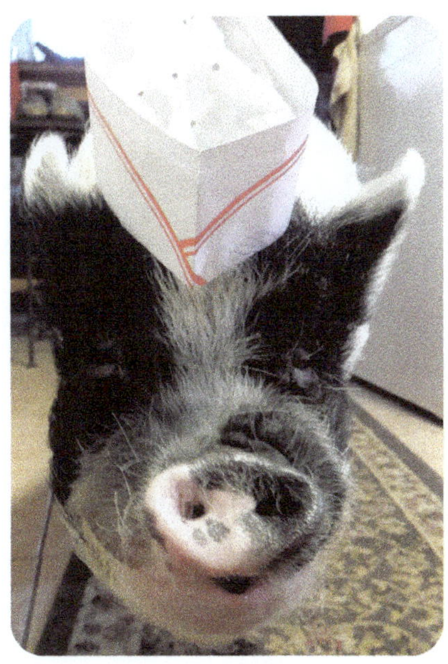

Every time that I took an order, I would eat the doughnuts before I put them in the bag for the customer. I like the jelly doughnuts the best! *Oink!* What is your favorite doughnut?

One year I got a summer job as a park ranger.

I wanted people to know how important it is to always be careful when in the forest. I have many, many friends that live in the forest. I have deer friends, birdie friends, chipmunk friends, and even bear friends, and a whole bunch of other friends that live in the forest. I want everyone to know that when they are using the forest and streams, which is where all my critter friends live, I would like them to be extra careful with campfires. It is very easy for a campfire to start, and once they start, it is very difficult to put out. Fires can seriously hurt my critter friends, and it can also burn their homes.

They would have nowhere else to go. *Oink!* That's bad! So please be careful when sharing the forest with my friends.

Do you like St. Patrick's Day? I oinken' do! Last year I auditioned to be the grand marshal pig for the parade, but they didn't pick me.

That's okay. I guess I was too good-looking, and they didn't want everyone watching me and not the other people in the parade. There is always next year! *Oink!*

I got a call from the police chief in town, and he asked me to help them look for a doggie who decided that he wanted to walk around town without his parents. *Oink!* Little doggie, there are way too many cars for you to be walking around without your parents. Since I am the piggie sheriff in town,

I went out and looked for the little doggie. Yay! *Oink!* I found him, and guess what? He didn't run away at all. He was playing hide-and-seek with his mom and dad, and he was hiding in his backyard. The problem was that he never told his mom and dad that he was playing hide-and-seek. *Oink!* Ha! Well, Sheriff Gerry the Pig found him, and I told him to tell his parents the next time he wants to play hide-and-seek. It's always good to tell your parents where you may be going so that they can keep an eye out for you.

One year, for Christmas, my mama and papa told me that they had a new Christmas lawn ornament for me in the backyard. I said, "Okay, *oink*." So before I went out, my papa put on my coat because it was a little chilly outside. Once I had my coat on, I ran outside to see my new ornament. I ran down the ramp and onto the lawn, and what did I see? A pink piggy that has a Santa hat like me.

I was so excited and happy to see the piggy lawn ornament. I always wanted one to decorate the outside of my house for Christmas. I wanted to name him Gerry Junior. But then I thought about it. There can only be one Gerry the Pig…and that's me! So instead I named him Christmas Pig. Do you like that name? Do you have a favorite outdoor decoration?

For Mother's Day, I went out to get my mama some roses. I like roses, but those thorns sure are sharp. *Oink!*

I love my mama, and you know what? For Halloween, my mama always gets me a pumpkin. As soon as my mama brings it home, I get all excited and happy to carve a pumpkin face out of the pumpkin. But there is one big problem. As soon as I put the pumpkin down on the grass and get ready to carve it ... I eat it. *Oink! Oink!*

I have an idea. Maybe next time I'll carve it then eat it. Ha! *Oink!*

I just love hanging in the backyard with my papa and mama and baby groundhog.

It's like having my own personal cabana. Hey! Get the waiter! My waiter is really my papa. Where's my favorite drink of apple juice and water? After I rest for a while, I sometimes help my papa do some yard work. I'm usually done helping him after picking up a branch or two.

Then after all my hard work, I always get a nice lunch of lettuce, carrots, blueberries, and celery.

Do you like to eat your vegetables? I hope so. They will make you big and strong like me! *Oink!*

I have plenty of squirrel friends in my backyard. Sometimes they tease me and eat peanuts right in front of me! Can you imagine that? When I start to slowly walk over to them, hoping that they would share, they run off. That's it! No more squirrel piggyback rides.

Oink!

When my mama eats breakfast, I make a funny face at her, and she shares a little bit of her breakfast with me.

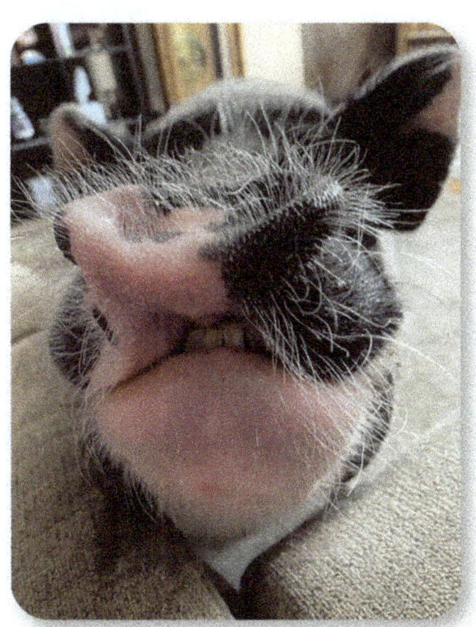

Maybe if you also make a funny face at your mama or papa during breakfast, you may just get an extra breakfast snack. *Oink!*

My papa took me for lunch yesterday and *oink*, was it good. I had a vegan burger with no cheese and no mayo. After eating my yummy burger, I went inside my house and took a nice nap and I dreamt of eating more burgers. *Oink*! Do you like to take naps like I do? *Oink!*

People always tell me that the only place that you can see sharks living a nice life with their friends is in the ocean, but just the other day, I saw the elusive and very rare Oink Shark in my backyard!

He was slowly walking around my backyard, looking for peanuts that the squirrels may have dropped. Some people say that Oink Shark looks like me. Do you think Oink Shark looks like me wearing a shark fin?

Well, I just finished eating dinner, and now it's time to go to bed. My papa and mama tuck me in nice. They give me my little stuffed animals, a nice fluffy pillow and a blanket, and I am off to sleep.

I always have happy piggy dreams when I go to sleep. I always dream about playing with my critter friends in the backyard. I hope that when you go to bed tonight, you have happy dreams also.

About the Author

Peter lives in New Jersey with his "son," Gerry the Pig, and his wife, Maria. He is retired from working with the federal government and spends most of his days during the summer with Gerry in the backyard. He has traveled to many other countries and has an extensive portfolio of photos of animals that he has encountered during his travels. During the year, Peter also transports injured and orphaned wildlife that are brought to the wildlife division of the Franklin Lakes Animal Hospital in Franklin Lakes, New Jersey, to various wildlife sanctuaries throughout New Jersey. These may include any animal—from a chipmunk to a hawk to a bald eagle.